THE
WISDOM
OF
Christina Rossetti

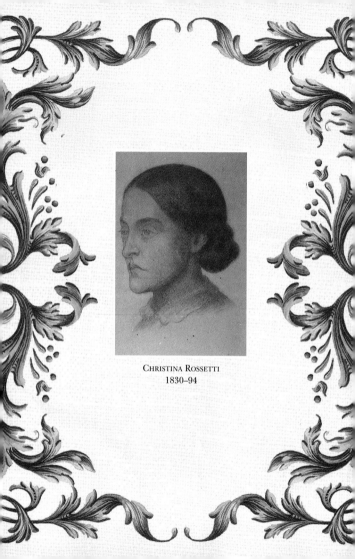

CHRISTINA ROSSETTI
1830–94

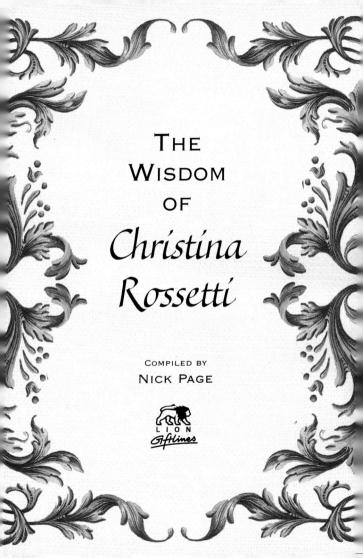

THE
WISDOM
OF
Christina
Rossetti

COMPILED BY
NICK PAGE

LION
Giftlines

This edition copyright © 1999 Lion Publishing

Published by
Lion Publishing plc
Sandy Lane West, Oxford, England
www.lion-publishing.co.uk
ISBN 0 7459 4078 1

First edition 1999
10 9 8 7 6 5 4 3 2 1 0

A catalogue record for this book is available
from the British Library

Typeset in 10/12 Baskerville
Printed and bound in Singapore

Designer: Philippa Jenkins
Artwork: Jane Thomson

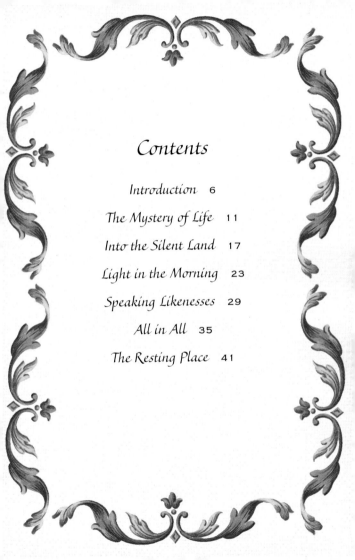

Contents

Introduction

'Fragments of her verse have been floating in the air,' wrote Ford Madox Ford of Christina Rossetti; 'almost every person at all lettered has carried about with him some little piece.'

Today, a century after Christina Rossetti's death, she remains one of the best-loved English poets, and poems like 'Goblin Market', 'In the Bleak Midwinter', 'Remember' and 'Up-Hill' still float around us.

Christina Rossetti was born in 1830, the youngest child of Gabriele Rossetti, an exiled Italian poet and philosopher, and his wife Frances, a translator and teacher. They were a talented family. Her sister Maria was an intelligent and devout woman, who later became a nun. Her two brothers were deeply involved in the art world, William writing art criticism and Dante Gabriel finding fame as one of the greatest painters of the Pre-Raphaelite Brotherhood.

But in the 1840s, Rossetti's world was turned upside-down, first by her father's mental collapse, which plunged her family into poverty, and then by her own nervous breakdown. There have been many theories about this illness, and the truth will never be known. Whatever the cause, her health remained frail from that time onwards.

As Rossetti emerged from her illness, she came under the influence of the emerging Anglo-Catholic movement led by Edward Pusey. For the rest of her life her strong Christian beliefs were the foundation-stone of her thinking and writing. From an early age she showed a remarkable talent for verse. In 1847 her first collection of poems was privately printed by her grandfather. The following year two of her poems were accepted by the *Athenaeum*, the most prestigious literary journal of the era.

She also became involved with the Pre-Raphaelite Brotherhood, a group of artists who had gathered around her brother Dante Gabriel. She contributed to their short-lived magazine, *The Germ*, and posed for some of Gabriel's most famous pictures.

At around this time Rossetti became engaged to James Collinson, but to her devastation the engagement ended when Collinson decided to dedicate himself to a life of celibacy in the Roman Catholic Church. Worse still, he later changed his mind, married and had a family. This was the first of three relationships which might in other circumstances have led to marriage. She was linked briefly with the painter John Brett, and much later with a linguist named Charles Bagot Cayley.

Despite the failure of these relationships and the sense of lost love which is found in much of her poetry, the image of Christina Rossetti as a timid spinster waiting at home for the man of her dreams is false. Admittedly, she was painfully shy and reserved, and, like so many women, was subject to strict Victorian conventions which forced women into a subservient role and frowned on any form of ambition or display. Nevertheless, she was certain of her own poetic ability.

She had to be, for it took many years before she found fame. Throughout the 1850s, despite producing some of her finest work, it was hard for her to attract the attention of any serious publisher. The breakthrough came in 1862 with her most famous poem, 'Goblin Market'. A magical tale of temptation, seduction and ultimate redemption, its sinuous rhythm, depth of imagination and powerful imagery make it one of the high points of Victorian poetry. The tale of Laura, seduced by the goblins into eating their fruit, and of Lizzie, who undergoes the ordeal to save her sister, was no doubt inspired by Rossetti's work at the St Mary Magdalene Home for Fallen Women at Highgate – a Christian institution which offered prostitutes the chance to turn their lives around and start again.

Rossetti's book, *Goblin Market and Other Poems*, was an immediate success, and established her as a unique voice in Victorian poetry. It was followed by *The Prince's Progress and Other Poems* and *Sing-Song*, a collection of nursery rhymes. She also published books of short stories, several volumes of devotional and theological works, and *Speaking Likenesses*, a dense and multi-layered book for children that reads like a darker, more threatening version of *Alice in Wonderland*.

There was always a dark side to Rossetti's writing, reflecting the hard times through which she struggled. Her brother Dante Gabriel died in 1882, after years of schizophrenia and drug dependency; her sister Maria died of cancer in 1876, and Christina herself suffered a series of debilitating and painful diseases, including Graves' Disease, a rare syndrome which affected her thyroid glands, drastically altered her appearance and brought her close to death.

The one factor that carried Rossetti through these

times was her faith. In many biographies, her deeply held Christian beliefs have been presented almost as a character defect. Even her brother William asserted that she was 'over-scrupulous', ceasing to 'ponder for herself whether a thing was true or not' and asking only 'whether it conformed to the Bible, as viewed by Anglo-Catholicism'.

At best, this is only partially true. She was a woman of powerful opinion, by no means ignorant of the major social issues of her time. She was an anti-vivisectionist and a passionate opponent of slavery; she campaigned on behalf of child prostitutes; she opposed Britain's imperial policies; she was a pacifist and she took a deep interest in the factory girls who worked brutally long hours in the match-making industry. At the same time, she was no ardent feminist. She opposed votes for women and perceived woman's role as a 'help-meet' for man.

Equally, her devotional writing – both poetry and prose – is far from a simple attempt to conform, but shows profound depth and spiritual insight. The modern mind might find it hard to appreciate how seriously she took her religion, but to Rossetti it was inspirational and challenging, as well as a support and consolation. It was the most important thing in her life.

There were, as for so many people, moments of doubt. Rossetti's natural shyness, combined with the intensity of her beliefs, sometimes made her seem austere. She could be acutely aware of hell and damnation and was prone to a certain Victorian morbidity. But she also sang joyously, and those who dismiss her faith as narrow or naïve understand little of the woman and even less of her beliefs.

By the final years of her life her reputation was such that after Tennyson's death she was seriously considered for the post of Poet Laureate. Were it not, one suspects, for the fact that she was female, she would have been honoured. As well as her friends in the Pre-Raphaelite circle, her poetry influenced writers such as Swinburne, Emily Dickinson and Gerard Manley Hopkins. Even Vincent van Gogh, working in London as a schoolteacher and lay preacher, ended a sermon with the first stanza of 'Up-Hill'.

In 1892 Rossetti contracted breast cancer. She underwent a mastectomy, which, although pronounced successful, could not stop the ultimate spread of the disease. She died in December 1894.

'A sprinkling of snow had remained on the ground,' a friend at her funeral recalled, 'and, as the closing words of the burial service were being read... the winter sunshine, gleaming through the leafless branches of some trees to the right, revealed in all their delicate tracery, while a robin sang.'

Christina Rossetti was a courageous woman and a great poet. Without doubt, her words will float on the air for years to come.

The Mystery of Life

*All the world over, visible things
typify things invisible.*

FROM *ANNUS DOMINI*

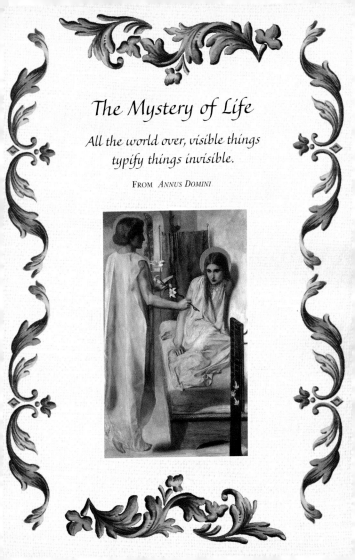

Visible Signs

The mystery of life, the mystery
  Of death, I see
Darkly as in a glass;
Their shadows pass,
And talk with me.

FROM 'MIRRORS OF LIFE AND DEATH'

There are sleeping dreams and waking dreams;
What seems is not always as it seems.

FROM 'A BALLAD OF BODING'

Mysteries and Miracles

Mysteries lie deeper than miracles: they address and they tax a higher faculty in whoso would apprehend them. Many a miracle could in its own day be estimated and attested by the senses: all mysteries ever have been and at this day continue inappreciable except by faith and love.

FROM *ANNUS DOMINI*

While knowledge runs apace, ignorance keeps ahead of knowledge: and all which the deepest students know proves to themselves, yet more convincingly than to others, that much more exists which still they know not.

FROM *SEEK AND FIND*

13

Bird or Beast?

Did any bird come flying
  After Adam and Eve,
When the door was shut against them
  And they sat down to grieve?

I think not Eve's peacock,
  Splendid to see,
And I think not Adam's eagle,
  But a dove maybe.

Did any beast come pushing
  Through the thorny hedge
Into the thorny thistly world
  Out from Eden's edge?

I think not a lion
  Though his strength is such;
But an innocent loving lamb
  May have done as much.

If the dove preached from her bough
  And the lamb from his sod,
The lamb and the dove
  Were preachers sent from God.

4

Judge not According to the Appearance

Lord, purge our eyes to see
Within the seed a tree,
  Within the glowing egg a bird,
   Within the shroud a butterfly:

Till taught by such, we see
Beyond all creatures thee,
  And hearken for thy tender word,
   And hear it, 'Fear not: it is I.'

One Loud Hymn

All voices of all things inanimate
Join with the song of Angels and the song
Of blessed Spirits, chiming with
Their Hallelujahs. One wind wakeneth
Across the sleeping sea, crisping along
The waves, and brushes through the great
Forests and tangled hedges, and calls out
Of rivers a clear sound,
And makes the ripe corn rustle on the ground,
And murmurs in a shell;
Till all their voices swell
Above the clouds in one loud hymn
Joining the song of Seraphim,
Or like pure incense circle round about
The walls of Heaven, or like a well-spring rise
In shady Paradise.

FROM 'TO WHAT PURPOSE IS THIS WASTE?'

Into the Silent Land

Must she then buy
no more such dainty fruit?
Must she no more
such succous pasture find,
Gone deaf and blind?

FROM 'GOBLIN MARKET'

Remember

Remember me when I am gone away,
  Gone far away into the silent land;
  When you can no more hold me by the hand,
Nor I half turn to go yet turning stay.
Remember me when no more day by day
  You tell me of our future that you planned:
  Only remember me; you understand
It will be late to counsel then or pray.
Yet if you should forget me for a while
  And afterwards remember, do not grieve:
  For if the darkness and corruption leave
  A vestige of the thoughts that once I had,
Better by far you should forget and smile
  Than that you should remember and be sad.

A Fair World though a Fallen

You tell me that the world is fair, in spite
  Of the old fall; and that I should not turn
  So to the grave, and let my spirit yearn
After the quiet of the long last night.
Have I then shut mine eyes against the light,
  Grief-deafened lest my spirit should discern?
  Yet how could I keep silence when I burn?
And who can give me comfort? – hear the right.
Have patience with the weak and sick at heart:
  Bind up the wounded with a tender touch.
  Comfort the sad, tear-blinded as they go:
For though I failed to choose the better part,
  Were it a less unutterable woe
If we should come to love this world too much?

Endure Hardness

A cold wind stirs the blackthorn
  To burgeon and to blow,
Besprinkling half-green hedges
  With flakes and sprays of snow.

Through coldness and through keenness,
  Dear hearts, take comfort so:
'Somewhere or other doubtless
  These make the blackthorn blow.

A Better Resurrection

I have no wit, no words, no tears;
  My heart within me like a stone
Is numbed too much for hopes or fears;
  Look right, look left, I dwell alone;
I lift mine eyes, but dimmed with grief
  No everlasting hills I see;
My life is in the falling leaf:
  O Jesus, quicken me.

My life is like a faded leaf,
  My harvest dwindled to a husk:
Truly my life is void and brief
  And tedious in the barren dusk;
My life is like a frozen thing,
  No bud nor greenness can I see:
Yet rise it shall – the sap of spring;
  O Jesus, rise in me.

My life is like a broken bowl,
  A broken bowl that cannot hold
One drop of water for my soul
  Or cordial in the searching cold;
Cast in the fire the perished thing;
  Melt and remould it, till it be
A royal cup for him, my king:
  O Jesus, drink of me.

Love is Strong as Death

I have not sought thee, I have not found thee,
  I have not thirsted for thee:
And now cold billows of death surround me,
Buffeting billows of death astound me –
  Wilt thou look upon, wilt thou see
  Thy perishing me?

'Yea, I have sought thee, yea, I have found thee,
  Yea, I have thirsted for thee,
Yea, long ago with love's bands I bound thee:
Now the everlasting arms surround thee –
  Through death's darkness I look and see
  And clasp thee to me.'

Light in the Morning

Tears once again
Refreshed her shrunken eyes,
Dropping like rain
After long sultry drouth.

FROM 'GOBLIN MARKET'

Night and Day

What though we should be deceived
By the friend that we love best?
All in this world have been grieved,
Yet many have found rest.
Our present life is as the night,
Our future as the morning light:
Surely the night will pass away,
And surely will uprise the day.

FROM 'HOPE IN GRIEF'

Greenness of Hope

O Lord Jesus Christ, lily of the valleys, clothe
us, I beseech thee, in whiteness of purity,
greenness of hope, fragrance of prayer...

<small>FROM *ANNUS DOMINI*</small>

The Song of Creation

Nothing is great on this side of the grave,
  Nor anything of any stable worth:
  Whatso is born from earth returns to earth:
Nothing we grasp proves half the thing we crave:
The tidal wave shrinks to the ebbing wave:
  Laughter is folly, madness lurks in mirth:
  Mankind sets off a-dying from the birth:
Life is a losing game, with what to save?
Thus I sat mourning like a mournful owl,
  And like a doleful dragon made ado,
    Companion of all monsters of the dark:
When lo! the light cast off its nightly cowl,
  And up to heaven flashed a carolling lark,
  And all creation sang its hymn anew.

FROM 'HEAVINESS MAY ENDURE FOR A NIGHT,
BUT JOY COMETH IN THE MORNING'

All is Love

Time flies, hope flags, life plies a wearied wing;
  Death following hard on life gains ground apace;
  Faith runs with each and rears an eager face,
Outruns the rest, makes light of everything,
Spurns earth, and still finds breath to pray and sing;
  While love ahead of all uplifts his praise,
  Still asks for grace and still gives thanks for grace,
Content with all day brings and night will bring.
Life wanes; and when love folds his wings above
  Tired hope, and less we feel his conscious pulse,
  Let us go fall asleep, dear friend, in peace:
  A little while, and age and sorrow cease;
  A little while, and life reborn annuls
Loss and decay and death, and all is love.

FROM 'MONNA INNOMINATA'

Advent

Earth grown old, yet still so green,
  Deep beneath her crust of cold
Nurses fire unfelt, unseen:
  Earth grown old.

  We who live are quickly told:
Millions more lie hid between
  Inner swathings of her fold.

When will fire break up her screen?
  When will life burst through her mould?
Earth, earth, earth, thy cold is keen,
  Earth grown old.

Speaking Likenesses

For there is no friend like a sister
In calm or stormy weather;
To cheer one on the tedious way,
To fetch one if one goes astray,
To lift one if one totters down,
To strengthen whilst one stands.

FROM 'GOBLIN MARKET'

Lives That Speak

A Christian is one whose smooth fair outer surface of manner covers and reveals a transparent depth of character and whose hidden man of the heart is fairer than any outward features.

FROM *LETTER AND SPIRIT*

Words are spoken: deeds and lives speak.

FROM *TIME FLIES*

I Am Not What I Have

I am not what I have nor what I do;
  But what I was I am, I am even I.

Therefore myself is that one only thing
  I hold to use or waste, to keep or give;
  My sole possession every day I live,
And still mine own despite Time's winnowing.

FROM 'THE THREAD OF LIFE'

His immutability is reflected in our identity:
as he cannot deny himself, so neither can we
deny ourselves. Rocks may fall on us, mountains
cover us; but under mountain and rock remains
the inextinguishable I.

FROM *THE FACE OF THE DEEP*

Not to Be First

Not to be first: how hard to learn
  That lifelong lesson of the past;
Line graven on line and stroke on stroke;
  But, thank God, learned at last.

So now in patience I possess
  My soul year after tedious year,
Content to take the lowest place,
  The place assigned me here.

Yet sometimes, when I feel my strength
  Most weak, and life most burdensome,
I lift mine eyes up to the hills
  From whence my help shall come:

Yea, sometimes still I lift my heart
  To the Archangelic trumpet-burst,
When all deep secrets shall be shown,
  And many last shall be first.

FROM 'THE LOWEST ROOM'

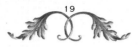

The Burning Issues

Now they are the wicked who stand callous
amidst the fears, torments, miseries of others;
not investigating human claims, not mourning
with them that mourn, not moving burdens
with one of their fingers, not heeding the
burning questions of their day, neighbourhood,
nay sometimes of their own hearths...

FROM *THE FACE OF THE DEEP*

The Lowest Place

Give me the lowest place: not that I dare
  Ask for that lowest place, but thou hast died
That I might live and share
  Thy glory by thy side.

Give me the lowest place: or if for me
  That lowest place too high, make one more low
Where I may sit and see
  My God and love thee so.

All in All

*In every creature is latent
a memorial of its creator.*

FROM *LETTER AND SPIRIT*

Love is Sweet

For what is knowledge duly weighed?
Knowledge is strong, but love is sweet;
Yea, all the progress he had made
Was but to learn that all is small
Save love, for love is all in all.

FROM 'THE CONVENT THRESHOLD'

Indifference

As lukewarmness stands between cold and
heat, so indifference stands between love and
hatred. If under the surface as well as upon
the surface the two series correspond, at once
light breaks in on our subject. For indifference,
so far as Holy Scripture instructs us, has no
part whatsoever in the divine being. God
Almighty we know is love; and it is revealed that
he can hate: but love and hatred alike preclude
indifference. Thus indifference appears to
involve absolute alienation from his image
and likeness.

FROM *THE FACE OF THE DEEP*

23

Untitled

If love is not worth loving,
   then life is not worth living,
   Nor aught is worth remembering
   but well forgot;
For store is not worth storing
   and gifts are not worth giving,
   If love is not;

   And idly cold is death-cold,
   and life-heat idly hot,
And vain is any offering
   and vainer our receiving,
   And vanity of vanities is all our lot.

   Better than life's heaving heart
   is death's heart unheaving,
   Better than the opening leaves
   are the leaves that rot,
For there is nothing worth
   achieving or retrieving,
   If love is not.

A Birthday

My heart is like a singing bird
  Whose nest is in a watered shoot;
My heart is like an apple tree
  Whose boughs are bent with thickset fruit;
My heart is like a rainbow shell
  That paddles in a halcyon sea;
My heart is gladder than all these
  Because my love is come to me.

Raise me a dais of silk and down;
  Hang it with vair* and purple dyes;
Carve it in doves and pomegranates,
  And peacocks with a hundred eyes;
Work it in gold and silver grapes,
  In leaves and silver fleurs-de-lys;
Because the birthday of my life
  Is come, my love is come to me.

squirrel fur, used in medieval times for trimming

Doubt and Love

St Thomas doubted.

Scepticism is a degree of unbelief:
equally therefore it is a degree of belief.
It may be a degree of faith.

St Thomas doubted, but simultaneously
he loved. Whence it follows that his case
was all along hopeful.

If we are spirit-broken by doubts of
our own, if we are half heart-broken by
a friend's doubts, let us beg faith for our
friend and for ourself; only still more
urgently let us beg love.

FROM *TIME FLIES*

The Resting Place

Pleasure past and anguish past,
Is it death or is it life?

Life out of death.

FROM 'GOBLIN MARKET'

Up-Hill

Does the road wind up-hill all the way?
   Yes, to the very end.
Will the day's journey take the whole long day?
   From morn to night, my friend.

But is there for the night a resting-place?
   A roof for when the slow dark hours begin.
May not the darkness hide it from my face?
   You cannot miss that inn.

Shall I meet other wayfarers at night?
   Those who have gone before.
Then must I knock, or call when just in sight?
   They will not keep you standing at that door.

Shall I find comfort, travel-sore and weak?
   Of labour you shall find the sum.
Will there be beds for me and all who seek?
   Yea, beds for all who come.

Sweeter than Death

Sweeter than a prayer-bell for a saint in dying,
Sweeter than a death-bell for a saint at rest,
Music struck in heaven with earth's faint replying
'Life is good, and death is good, for Christ is best.'

FROM 'CHRISTMAS CAROLS'

Christmas Carols

Christmas hath a darkness
  Brighter than the blazing noon,
Christmas hath a chillness
  Warmer than the heat of June,
Christmas hath a beauty
  Lovelier than the world can show,
For Christmas bringeth Jesus
  Brought for us so low.

FROM *TIME FLIES*

Our God, Heaven cannot hold him
  Nor earth sustain;
Heaven and earth shall flee away
  When he comes to reign:
In the bleak midwinter
  A stable-place sufficed
The Lord God Almighty
  Jesus Christ.

FROM 'A CHRISTMAS CAROL'

The Tender Voice

A dimness of a glory glimmers here
  Through veils and distance from the space remote,
  A faintest far vibration of a note
Reaches to us and seems to bring us near;
Causing our face to glow with braver cheer,
  Making the serried mist to stand afloat,
  Subduing langour with an antidote,
And strengthening love almost to cast out fear:
Till for one moment golden city walls
  Rise looming on us, golden walls of home,
Light of our eyes until the darkness falls;
  Then through the outer darkness burdensome
I hear again the tender voice that calls,
  'Follow me hither, follow, rise and come.'

FROM 'THEY DESIRE A BETTER COUNTRY'

30

A Blessing

Oh my heart's heart, and you who are to me
  More than myself myself, God be with you,
  Keep you in strong obedience leal* and true
To him whose noble service setteth free,
Give you all good we see or can foresee,
  Make your joys many and your sorrows few,
  Bless you in what you bear and what you do,
Yea, perfect you as he would have you be.

FROM 'MONNA INNOMINATA'

* *loyal, honest*

Select Bibliography

Verses (privately printed), 1847
Goblin Market and Other Poems, 1862
The Prince's Progress and Other Poems, 1866
Commonplace and Other Short Stories, 1870
Sing-Song, 1871
Annus Domini, 1874
Speaking Likenesses, 1874
Collected Poems, 1875
Seek and Find, 1879
A Pageant and Other Poems, 1881
Called to be Saints, 1881
Letter and Spirit, 1883
Time Flies, A Reading Diary, 1885
The Face of the Deep, 1892

Acknowledgments

cover, 1: An Angel Playing a Harp by John Mellush Strudwick; Christies Images
2: FIT68499 Christina Rossetti (drawing) by Dante Gabriel Rossetti
(1828–82); Fitzwilliam Museum, University of Cambridge/Bridgeman Art
Library, London/New York
11: Ecce Ancilla Domini by Dante Gabriel Rossetti; © Tate Gallery, London
17: BAL7779 Day Dream, 1880 by Dante Gabriel Rossetti; Victoria &
Albert Museum, London/Bridgeman Art Library, London/New York
23: The Lament by Sir Edward Coley Burne-Jones; The William Morris
Gallery, Walthamstow, London
25: BAL13776 The Soul of the Rose, 1908 (oil on canvas) by John William
Waterhouse (1849–1917); Private Collection/Julian Hartnoll, London/
Bridgeman Art Library, London/New York
29: The Woman in Yellow by Dante Gabriel Rossetti; © Tate Gallery, London
35: BAL2561 The Light of the World by William Holman Hunt (1827–1910);
Keble College, Oxford/Bridgeman Art Library, London/New York
41: The Morning of the Resurrection by Sir Edward Coley Burne-Jones;
Christies Images
47: The Golden Staircase by Sir Edward Coley Burne-Jones; © Tate
Gallery, London